YUMMY!

Good Food Makes Me Strong!

by **Shelley Rotner** and **Sheila M. Kelly**

photographs by **Shelley Rotner**

Holiday House / New York

To Sheila, for her insight and patience
in the creation of this book
—S. R.

To Eliza and Iris Haynes and to Sara Haynes, their mother,
who did helpful fieldwork for this book
—S. M. K.

The source of nutritional information in this book is the United States Department of Agriculture website,
where links may be found that advise on what to feed your child and what to avoid.
Information we provide in the tips sections comes from nutritionally conscious mothers
of young children and is in accord with USDA recommendations.

Text copyright © 2013 by Shelley Rotner and Sheila M. Kelly
Photographs copyright © 2013 by Shelley Rotner
All Rights Reserved
HOLIDAY HOUSE is registered in the U.S. Patent and Trademark Office.
Printed and Bound in October 2012 at Kwong Fat Offset Printing Co. Ltd., DongGuan City, China.
The text typeface is Univers.
www.holidayhouse.com
First Edition
1 3 5 7 9 10 8 6 4 2

Library of Congress Cataloging-in-Publication Data
Rotner, Shelley.
Yummy! : good food makes me strong! / by Shelley Rotner and Sheila M. Kelly ; photographs by Shelley Rotner.
p. cm.
ISBN 978-0-8234-2426-9 (hardcover)
1. Nutrition—Juvenile literature. 2. Food—Juvenile literature. 3. Children—Nutrition—Juvenile literature.
I. Kelly, Sheila M. II. Rotner, Shelley, ill. III. Title.
QP141.R68 2013
612.3—dc23
2012016564

Good food makes me **strong**!

Breakfast Time!

Yummy pancakes!

I stir the oatmeal.

Add fruit puree or applesauce to pancake, waffle, or muffin mix, allowing for additional moisture.

I pour the milk.

I like milk.

I can spread cream cheese
on my bagel.

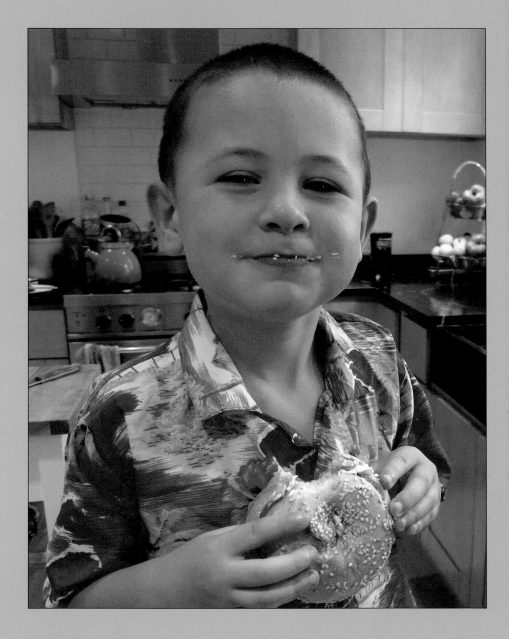

Yummy eggs!

Good food makes me **strong**!

Choose whole grain cereals and breads. Use low fat spreads.
Limit sugar. Check with your doctor about choosing low fat milk for your child.

Come have a snack!

Yummy fruit!

Make fresh fruit part of the daily diet.
Pieces of fruit make excellent snacks.

I make shakes.

Make shakes using yogurt and fresh fruit.

Mixing nuts, raisins, and seeds is fun!
Cheese sticks!
Yummy yogurt!

I make my own pops.

Make your own pops using yogurt and fresh fruit purees.
Check the sugar content in yogurt.

Good food makes me **strong**!

Lunch is ready!

I like to eat what I help make.

I like to dip.

Involve kids in preparing and cooking foods. Make dips with yogurt or different beans or avocado so kids can dip their vegetables.

Yummy soup!

Sandwiches!
Pizza!

Wraps are fun!

Good food makes me **strong**!

Avoid high fat luncheon meats such as bologna and salami.
Choose low salt breads and crackers.

I help pick the apples.

My mom reads the box.

We get lots of vegetables.

READ THE LABELS!
Buy as few processed foods as possible.
Look for foods without chemical additives and with low salt.
Rinse canned foods such as beans and vegetables in water to reduce the amount of salt.
Avoid canned fruit packed with extra sugar.
Avoid foods containing trans fats or hydrogenated fats.

Yummy blueberries!

I picked a carrot.

This is a giant pepper!

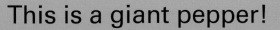

Look how big the lettuce grew!

Encourage kids to learn where food comes from and to grow their own.

We grew the vegetables for the salad.

I made the salad.

Good food makes me **strong**!

Dinner's ready!

Yummy burgers!

Rice and beans
and broccoli!

I like chicken.

I can shuck the corn.

Broil, grill, roast, or bake instead of fry. Make beans and peas a part of the diet.

Using chopsticks is fun!

We love spaghetti!

Yummy!

Good food makes
me **strong**!

Buy pastas that are high in protein, legumes, and multigrains.
Make pesto using walnuts and fresh or frozen spinach or peas to increase vegetable intake.

Yummy! Treats!

Include nuts and seeds in your family's diet. They are good sources of protein. Bake your own sweets leaving out the salt and reducing the amount of sugar. Ice cream or frozen yogurt can be a healthy treat in a diet that is rich in fresh fruits, vegetables, and proteins.

Good food makes me **strong**!

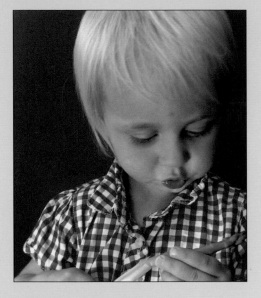

More Helpful Tips

Encourage kids to help prepare food.

Offer water rather than juice with all snacks and meals.

Serve children small portions.

Offer a new food at the beginning of a meal as a taste before serving it on a plate.

Separate the foods on a child's plate, though the child may choose to mix them.

Eat together to make sharing a meal a pleasant experience!

Be a healthy role model for your children.

The United States Department of Agriculture created MyPlate to illustrate the five food groups using a familiar mealtime visual: a place setting. The MyPlate website features practical information and tips to help Americans build healthier diets: **choosemyplate.gov**